TALES TOO TICKLISH TO TELL

BLOOM COUNTY BOOKS BY BERKE BREATHED

LOOSE TAILS

'TOONS FOR OUR TIMES

PENGUIN DREAMS and Stranger Things

BLOOM COUNTY BABYLON:
Five Years of Basic Naughtiness

BILLY AND THE BOINGERS BOOTLEG

TALES TOO TICKLISH TO TELL

BLOOM COUNTY

Tales Too Ticklish to Tell

BERKE BREATHED

LITTLE, BROWN AND COMPANY · BOSTON · TORONTO

FIRST EDITION

Bloom County is syndicated by
the Washington Post Writers Group

Library of Congress Cataloging-in-Publication Data

Breathed, Berke.
   [Bloom County. Selections]
   Tales too ticklish to tell / Berke Breathed. — 1st ed.
     p. cm.
   "A Bloom County book."
   ISBN 0-316-10735-2 (pbk.)
   I. Title. II. Title: Bloom County.
PN6728.B57B735 1988   88-9302
741.5'973 — dc 19   CIP

A full-color art print of Mr. Bush and Mr. Opus in Barbados
is available from: Guy Glenn Graphics, P.O. Box 3953,
Evergreen, Colorado 80439 • (303) 674-8667
Call or write for details.

Cover art by Berke Breathed and Jim Newport

10   9   8   7   6   5   4   3   2   1

WAK

Published simultaneously in Canada
by Little, Brown & Company (Canada) Limited
Printed in the United States of America

INTRODUCTION
by MIKHAIL GORBACHEV
TRANSLATED BY KALEVI LEONOF

When presented with the material that was to be the contents of this cartoon book, I was at once surprised and amused. The thin cat Bill and his companion Opus the Arctic Bird were not the usual heroes of American literature! But upon reconsideration, I am not so surprised.

I have read several American books, including *Huckleberry Finn* by the southern writer Mark Twain. The themes of the lone individual in his struggle with the imposed injustices of his oppressors has been dealt with extensively in such works. Indeed, it is in the relationship between Opus and Bill that I also see a parallel situation with Huckleberry Finn and the escaping Negro slave-laborer Jim. Both Bill and the slave Jim have experienced the social degradations of a system unresponsive to the particular needs of its citizens. Both characters are forced to turn to rely on others—saviors as such—to deliver them from the consequences of an injust situation. When Opus the Bird explains to his friend Bill that he is probably being exploited by his new romantic companion UN Ambassador Jeane Kirkpatrick, we can readily see a similar struggle when Huckleberry saved the slave Jim from drowning in the great Mississippi river.

The dialectics of Bloom County are such: the more oppressive and dangerous is the situation, the more we need the warm embrace of others. I salute and warmly recommend this cartoon book to all Americans, especially those "drowning in the great Mississippi river," as it were.

It is here where I must be forthright and admit that the publishers of this volume have successfully appealed to my schoolboy vanity by requesting a modest "doodle" cartoon. As the reader will plainly detect, the Pentagon will be sad to see that I will not be leaving my governmental duties for a new career in the art profession anytime soon!

WASHINGTON, D.C.
DECEMBER 8, 1987

1

YER HOME!

MILO, IF I'M EVER FORCED TO SHARE ANOTHER BED WITH HIM AGAIN, **SHOOT ME.**

THE GUY HAS EVEN MORE VIVIDLY LASCIVIOUS DREAMS ABOUT VANNA WHITE THAN **ME**.

I'M GONNA BE EMOTIONALLY SCARRED FOR THE REST OF MY ★@#% **LIFE!**

WHAT HAPPENED?

APPARENTLY I LICKED HIS NOSE AT AROUND 4 a.m..

BILL...PLEASE TRY TO GRASP WHAT I'M ABOUT TO EXPLAIN...

NABISCO WANTS TO BUY THE RIGHTS TO YOUR SONG "U STINK BUT I ♡ U" AND THEN REWRITE IT AS A TV JINGLE FOR "WHEAT THINS." THEY'LL MAKE YOU A MULTIMILLIONAIRE.

DID YOU GET ALL THAT, OL' BUDDY?

SELL OUT!!

HE'S GOT IT!

THAT'S RIGHT...BILL HAS AGREED TO SELL NABISCO ONE OF HIS BOINGERS SONGS AS A TV JINGLE FOR $12 MILLION.

NO!

YOU'VE MADE US RICH?!

STEVE, YOU GAVE UP YOUR SUBSIDIARY PERCENTAGE WHEN YOU REWROTE THEIR CONTRACTS IN JAIL LAST WEEK.

YOU'VE SOLD US OUT?!

THROTTLE THROTTLE THROTTLE

3

ANOTHER DISPATCH HAS ARRIVED FROM TOP BOINGER BILL THE CAT, IN L.A....

NO OBSCENITIES OR SPITTING IN STUDIO

"DEAR FELLOW ROCKERS: BILLY AND THE BOINGERS WILL NOW BE A CRITIC-PLEASING, SOCIALLY CONSCIOUS POP BAND WITH LEFTIST OVERTONES. SIGNED, YOUR LEADER, BILL"

THUS THE BAND'S CHIEF LYRICIST SET OFF TO PURSUE THIS STARTLING NEW MUSICAL DIRECTION... ONLY TO DISCOVER WHAT GROUPS LIKE U2 ALREADY KNOW:

...NOTHING RHYMES WITH "NICARAGUA"

...AGUA... BHAGWAN... OH, TO HECK WITH IT...

HE WHAT?

BILL WROTE FROM MALIBU AND ORDERED THE BOINGERS TO BECOME SOCIALLY CONSCIOUS.

A POLITICAL BAND? I'LL KILL HIM!

NOW, STEVE... I SUSPECT HE'S SUFFERING ENOUGH ALREADY.

WHY, JUST IMAGINE THE WRENCHING MORAL CRISIS THESE EARTHY, LEFTIST ROCK STARS LIKE BILL MUST FACE WHEN THEY BECOME FILTHY RICH.

HOW DO THEY DEAL WITH IT?

SNIFF.

SUPPORT THE HOMELESS

HODGE-PODGE! IT'S HERE! OUR REVIEW IN "TIME"!!

"WITH THEIR LATEST RECORD, THE NEWLY RELEVANT BOINGERS WEAVE TRANCELIKE MELODIES THAT SLIP OVER THE TRANSOM OF SOCIAL CONSCIOUSNESS AND INSINUATE THEMSELVES INTO YOUR DREAMS."

YEAH, BUT DO WE KICK BUTT?

READ IT AGAIN.

I'M NOT SURE HOW THE WEDDING SNUCK UP ON ME! THERE'RE STILL SO MANY QUESTIONS

LIKE.. WHAT ABOUT LOLA'S CAREER? WILL SHE WORK?

TRANSLATION: "WILL SHE HAVE THE TIME TO COOK AND CARE FOR ME?"

...DO WE WANT TO RAISE A FAMILY?

"DO I HAVE TO START ACTING MY AGE?"

AND FOR CRYING OUT LOUD... DO WE KNOW EACH OTHER WELL ENOUGH YET?

"WILL SHE DIVORCE ME AFTER SEEING HOW I LOOK AT SIX IN THE MORNING?"

THIS IS MOVING TOO FAST! I DON'T WANT A BACHELOR PARTY!!

YOU'LL HAVE A GREAT TIME. IT'S ALL SET UP IN THE STORM CELLAR.

OPEN UP! IT IS I... WITH THE DOOMED, SOON-TO-BE-ENSLAVED BACHELOR.. HERE FOR ONE LAST EVENING OF WILD AND LASCIVIOUS MALE REVELRY!!

DID YA GET WHAT I TOLD YA?

ALL WE COULD FIND WAS A 1964 "MARY POPPINS" OUTTAKE OF JULIE ANDREWS SAYING THE "S"-WORD.

THAT'S A STAG FILM?!

HEY...JUST THINK ABOUT IT! I GET GOOSE BUMPS!

IT'S TRUE. HE DOES.

I'D LIKE TO THANK YOU ALL FOR BOTH THIS PARTY AND THE GIFT OF THE ANATOMICALLY CORRECT LIFE-SIZE INFLATABLE DOLL. I'M TOUCHED.

YES, YOU'VE DONE SO WELL IN REMINDING ME OF ALL THOSE GREAT ASPECTS ABOUT THE SINGLE LIFE I'M LEAVING BEHIND:

LONELINESS... SELFISHNESS... TAWDRY ENCOUNTERS... V.D. ... AIDS... IMMATURE AND ANIMALISTIC ATTITUDES TOWARD WOMEN...

I'LL MISS IT ALL SO MUCH!

IS HE BEING SARCASTIC?

8

9

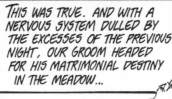

I'M... GETTING HITCHED TODAY!

THIS WAS TRUE. AND WITH A NERVOUS SYSTEM DULLED BY THE EXCESSES OF THE PREVIOUS NIGHT, OUR GROOM HEADED FOR HIS MATRIMONIAL DESTINY IN THE MEADOW...

WEDDING AHEAD

...STOPPING ONLY BRIEFLY FOR A FEW WORDS FROM THE BRIDE'S MOTHER.

WHISPER WHISPER

HOWEVER, THE BRIBE WAS INEFFECTIVE. THE MARRIAGE WAS A GO!

200! 275!

HELLO, LOLA. WELL... I GUESS THIS IS IT! THE BEGINNING OF THE GREAT ADVENTURE!

I'M SO HAPPY!

I COULD STILL RUN OFF TO BOLIVIA WITH A BIKER.

INTO THE ABYSS.

YOU LOOK HANDSOME.

YOU LOOK BEAUTIFUL.

HE LOOKS LIKE A TOADSTOOL.

SHE LOOKS BEAUTIFUL.

...I PRONOUNCE YOU WATERFOWL AND WIFE. YOU MAY KISS THE BRIDE.

THIS IS IT, BUCKAROO. JUMP UP HERE AND PLANT 'EM.

KISS? BUT I'VE NEVER KISSED ANYONE BEFORE! I WAS SAVING MYSELF FOR MARRIAGE.

...WHICH, GENTLE READERS, OUR HERO *DID*. WHAT HAPPENED NEXT WOULD NOT ONLY AFFECT FUTURE EVENTS IN WAYS UNIMAGINED, BUT WOULD ALSO HIGHLIGHT A MARITAL PROBLEM HERETOFORE UNDISCOVERED...

...INCOMPATIBLE NOSES. LOLA WAS UNDAMAGED. THE GROOM, HOWEVER, WAS OUT COLD.

OW.

CONTINUED—

IS HE DELIRIOUS?

YES. AND FROM WHAT HE'S MUMBLING...

..I'D SAY HE'S HALLUCINATING ABOUT MARRIED LIFE WITH YOU TWENTY YEARS IN THE FUTURE...

≥GROAN≤...COOK DINNER... CHANGE THE DIAPERS... CLEAN THE MICRO-LASER OVEN...

WAAA!

..NO, LOLA...FRANKLY, I CAN'T SAY THAT PRESIDENT STEINEM HAD A PARTICULARLY HELPFUL INFLUENCE ON THIS COUNTRY!!

WORLD'S BEST HOUSE-HUSBAND

MICRO LASER COOKER

MARRIED LIFE IN 2007 A.D.

OH, LOLA? DEAR? WOULD YOU MIND IF I WENT WITH STEVE DALLAS AND HUNG OUT WITH THE GUYS AT THE CORNER COCAINE BAR?

NO! OUR 23RD CHILD IS DUE AT THE OSCAR MAYER SURROGATE TEST-TUBE EMBRYO FARM... GO PICK HIM UP!

BOY... STEVE'S GONNA REALLY THINK I'M WHIPPED.

SORRY. CAN'T GO.

SHE'S GOT YOU WHIPPED, BLOBBO.

2007 A.D. ...

STEVE...YOU'RE STILL A BACHELOR AT 48... AM I MISSING ANYTHING?

NO SMOKIN ZONE

ZUDO'S SUBSTANCE TAVERN

I MEAN.. AFTER TWENTY YEARS OF MARRIAGE TO LOLA, I'M SUFFOCATING!

NO SMOKIN ZONE

ZUDO'S SUBSTANCE TAVERN

JEEZ! I GOT 23 GENETICALLY PURE, TUBE-GROWN KIDS! I NEED ADVICE!

ZBLAT!

ZUDO'S SUBSTANCE TAVERN

YOU'RE THE LAST BUDDY I'VE GOT, STEVE!

DON'T FORGET TO CLEAN UP YOUR ASHES, SIR!

CIG POLICE

14

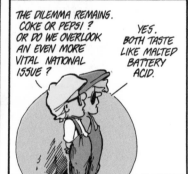

17

DAY FOUR: "OLD PHOTOS SURFACE"...

DESPITE THE MEDIA'S LIES, MISS DROCK IS A FORMER MODEL AND OCCASIONAL ACTRESS. IN OTHER WORDS, SHE'S A BUBBLING CAULDRON OF WICKED LUSTFULNESS.

MY CLIENT WOULD NEVER RISK THE PEOPLE'S FAITH BY INVOLVING HIMSELF WITH A WOMAN ANY MORE RESPECTABLE THAN THAT.

SEE THE NEW "TIME"?

AAIGH!!

SISTER EDITH DROCK AT HER CALCUTTA ORPHANAGE IN 1982.

DAY FIVE: "THE FALL"...

IT'S OVER, BILL, OL' BUDDY... YOUR REPUTATION IS FATALLY BESMIRCHED WITH RESPECTABILITY.

YOUR CAREER WITH THE BOINGERS IS SHOT. PREPARE AN EMOTIONAL PRESS STATEMENT...

SIGH

..BE SURE TO POINT OUT WHO'S TO BLAME FOR YOUR DOWNFALL: THE MEDIA...THE PUBLIC... THE MUSIC BUSINESS... LIBERALISM...THE COURTS... COMMUNISM...CHOLESTEROL... UH...

IGNORE THAT! BILL?... IGNORE THAT!

YOURSELF!!

ANATOMY OF A SCANDAL, DAY SIX: "THE LONG RIDE BACK HOME."...

YES, YOU REALLY BLEW IT. EMBARRASSED YOURSELF. DASHED YOUR DREAMS. DISAPPOINTED THE WORLD...

AND WORST OF ALL, EVERYONE INVOLVED SUFFERED IN THE END...

...ALMOST EVERYONE.

TAKE ONE EDITH DROCK PEPSI ENDOR

MY ANXIETY CLOSET... A BASTION OF METAPHORS AND METAPHYSICS ... OF MY FOIBLES AND FEARS, BOTH SUBTLE AND SUBLIME.

AND NOT SO SUBLIME.

EELS.

A *SCARY* ANXIETY TONIGHT, BINKLEY BOY! WE'LL BE BRINGING OUT *ALL* THE DEMOCRATIC PRESIDENTIAL CANDIDATES!

NO.. ANYTHING BUT THEM... NOT *THEM* !! NOT *THEM* !! NOT...

UH...

WHO ARE THEY?

HAVEN'T THE FOGGIEST. THAT'S THE SCARY PART.

CRIME.. DRUGS.. ADULTERY.. DEBT... IT'S *ETHICS*, BINKLEY... AMERICA IS HAVING A CRISIS IN PLAIN, SIMPLE ...

...ETHICS.

AWRIGHT! AWRIGHT! STOP HOUNDING ME!!

YES! YES, I TOOK *TWO* "USA TODAY"S FROM THE STAND AFTER PAYING FOR ONLY ONE! ...A MORAL SLIP... AN ETHICAL FUMBLE... BUT I'M OFF TO PAY THE EXTRA DOUGH RIGHT NOW!!

YEP. THE COUNTRY IS GOING TO HELL IN A HANDBASKET.

GOT A QUARTER?

WHADDYA THINK, MR. JONES? IS THE SCANDALOUS BEHAVIOR OF OUR LEADERS AFFECTING THE ETHICAL STANDARDS OF OUR SOCIETY?

CAN'T TALK, MILO. I'M MINING MY GARDEN WITH EXPLOSIVES.

THIS SHOULD KEEP MRS. GILLCREST'S DOG FROM LIFTING HIS LEG ON MY BEETS AGAIN.

FRANKLY, IF HART CAN DIDDLE A BLONDE, I CAN SMOKE A SCHNAUZER.

SEE?! SEE?!

SO THE ETHICAL DILEMMA YOU PRESENT ME IS WHETHER I, AS A FUTURE MAN OF SCIENCE AND KNOWLEDGE, WOULD OR WOULDN'T ACCEPT HUGE GRANTS FROM THE GOVERNMENT TO DEVELOP WEAPONS CAPABLE OF DESTROYING MAN AND ALL HIS KNOWLEDGE.

RIGHT.

HMM.

HMM. HMM HMM.

FORGET IT.

STILL THINKING.

DEPRESSED BY THE STATE OF PERSONAL ETHICS IN AMERICA, THE "BLOOM PICAYUNE" INTERN CONTEMPLATES A MAJOR STORY...

Ethics Desk

QUESTIONS: EXACTLY **WHO** IS BEING UNETHICAL OUT THERE, AND **WHAT** SORT OF UNETHICAL THINGS ARE THEY DOING?

ETHICALLY SPEAKING, THIS REPORTER'S RESPONSIBILITY IS CLEAR:

VITAL SUPPLIES →

GOTTA PEEK IN A FEW O' DEM WINDOWS!

23

THE WHOLE THING STARTED WHEN THE YOUNG INTERN AT THE "BLOOM PICAYUNE" ("CHRONICLE OF THE NEGLECTED TRUTH") SNIFFED OUT A HOT LEAD...

CUTTER JOHN IS PLANNING A SPECTACULAR DEMONSTRATION TODAY AT ELK'S HOLLOW. KEEP IT UNDER YOUR HAT...

HE DIDN'T.

I WANT PICTURES!! I WANT EMOTION! NO TELLING WHAT INSPIRING FEAT THIS DISABLED GUY HAS IN MIND!!

HEADLINES WERE PREPARED FOR ANY CONTINGENCY...

"HANDICAPPED MAN PARACHUTES NUDE INTO PICKLE BARREL TO PROVE HE'S AS ABLE AS ANYONE"

GOOD. THAT SINGS.

THE NEWS TEAM— SUCH AS IT WAS— SET OUT FOR THE RUMORED EVENT...

OKAY! THE MEDIA'S HERE! WHAT'S THE STUNT?

TO ATTRACT HUGE NUMBERS OF FROGS BY MAKING LOUD VULGAR SOUNDS.

THBBT! FRRRT! THBPPT!!

THAT'S IT?! THAT'S INSPIRING?

IT WAS, ACTUALLY... BUT ONLY TO THE FROGGING INDUSTRY. BUT, NEVER ONE TO DISAPPOINT, CUTTER JOHN ATTEMPTED SEVERAL WHEELIES FOR INSPIRATIONAL EFFECT. ALAS, THE PRESS HAD LEFT, WHICH WAS JUST AS WELL, CONSIDERING THE QUALITY OF THE WHEELIES.

WHOA.

WHOA!

WATCH IT!

HE'S JUST GETTING WHAT HE DESERVES.

WHO?

GARY HART. I SAY NAIL THE DUDE.

WHY?

THE MAN'S GOT NO DISCRETION! I HOPE THEY THROW HIS BONES TO THOSE LEERING JACKALS OF THE PRESS!

STEVE... YOU'RE SO SEXY WHEN YOU'RE SELF-RIGHTEOUS...

SMOOCH!

SMACK!

THE CANDIDATE FOR THE ROTARY CLUB TREASURER RACE IS SQUEEZING MARY LOU MCDERP.

WHY, HE'LL BE SQUEEZING THE "CHARMIN" NEXT!!

MILO! IT'S MY DAD...

HE'S BEEN IN THERE WATCHING FUNDAMENTALLY ORAL BILL ON TV ALL DAY! ALL DAY!!

HE'S AT THE END OF HIS ROPE, MILO... HE'S VERY VULNERABLE!...

I...I SEE A MAN OUT THERE...HE'S CRYING OUT FOR HELP...HE HAS A LEAKING...A LEAKING...KIDNEY...

NO! FUEL PUMP! FUEL PUMP!!

SON...LAST NIGHT IN FRONT OF THE TV...I BECAME A BORN-AGAIN FUNDAMENTALIST.

YEAH. NOTICED THE HAIR.

THINGS ARE BECOMING CLEARER...FUNDAMENTAL TRUTHS ARE SUDDENLY REVEALING THEMSELVES AT ANY GIVEN MOMENT!...I...I...

HOLD IT! I FEEL ANOTHER ONE COMING ON...STAND BY!

SON, JIMMY CARTER'S GOING TO HELL FOR GIVING AWAY THE PANAMA CANAL.

YEAH, WELL, DOWN THE HATCH.

SON? I WONDER IF YOU COULD GIVE ME A HAND WITH MY "ORAL BILL FUNDAMENTALIST WORKBOOK"...

BRYLCREEM

CLEAN GUMS

YOU STUDY THE BIBLE PRETTY HARD IN SUNDAY SCHOOL, DON'T YOU, SON?

SURE.

THEN WHERE EXACTLY IN REVELATIONS DOES IT SAY, "THE BEAST SHALL REVEAL ITSELF AND HE SHALL BE NORMAN LEAR"?

UH, NO GOOD, DAD.

WHAT? TRICK QUESTION? IS IT "DR. RUTH"?

29

WELL, CAPTAIN... I GUESS I WON'T BE GOING WHERE NO MAN HAS GONE BEFORE ANYMORE...

THIS IS RIDICULOUS. YOU **HAVE** TO LEAVE?

THEY DIDN'T GIVE ME MUCH CHOICE.

WHAT'RE YA GONNA DO? WHERE YA GONNA GO?

WELL, THE SKINNY-DIPPIN' WOLF WOMEN OF PLANET HEINEKEN OFFERED ME A JOB AS TOWEL BOY AT THEIR NUDE NITROGEN-PUDDING BATHS.

OH, THAT'S NOT TRUE.

YA GOTTA DREAM, MAN.

EXCUSE ME. DOES THIS BUS GO TO A NEW AND HOPEFUL LIFE BEYOND THE SUNNY HORIZON, LEAVING BEHIND A WORLD OF PAIN AND PREJUDICE AND FRIENDS FOREVER FAILED?

WITH A STOP IN TOLEDO.

THANKS.

VROOOM!

TRAILWAYS

ORAL BILL WEEKNIGHTS

U JUST LEFT BLOOM COUNTY

WHAT'S THAT, YOU ASK? HOW DID WE RATIONALIZE HOUNDING THAT SINNER OPUS OUT OF TOWN?

WELL, BROTHER PORTNOY AND MYSELF WERE READING SCRIPTURE LAST TUESDAY, AND WE CAME ACROSS "LET HE WHO IS WITHOUT SIN CAST THE FIRST STONE."...

RIGHT, BROTHER PORTNOY?

RIGHT. SO WE **CAST** THAT FIRST MUTHA!

GAZONGAS

OPUS IS GONE. BANISHED... HOUNDED OUT BY A FRIGHTENED FEW. BLOOM COUNTY IS NOW SAFE FROM THE THREAT OF RAMPANT, UNBRIDLED PENGUIN LUST...

THE QUESTION REMAINS: SHOULD ANYONE HAVE DONE MORE TO PREVENT THIS?

QUACK.

RIBBET!

THE QUESTION REMAINS--

MAYBE! JUST POSSIBLY MAYBE!!

HEY.. YOU GUYS ARE MISSING YOUR "ORAL BILL SHOW."

NAW. DON'T WATCH HIM ANYMORE. WE WERE ONCE BORN AGAIN...

BUT NOW WE'RE BORN THRICE.

THREE'S A CHARM!

IT HAPPENED VERY SUDDEN-LIKE...

WE WERE SITTIN' THERE WATCHIN' PHIL DONAHUE AND SUDDENLY--

WHACKO! OPEN-MINDEDNESS!

YOU'VE GOT TO REACH OPUS! TELL HIM EVERYTHING'S BACK TO NORMAL AROUND HERE!!

I FIGURE HE'S REACHED TULSA...

HELLO? TULSA BUS STATION? HAVE YOU SEEN A SHORT FAT GUY WITH A BIG NOSE COME THROUGH? HE WAS PROBABLY EATING OR CRYING...

WHAT?! HE BOUGHT A ONE-WAY TICKET TO OBLIVION?! YOU GOTTA STOP HIM, MAN! QUICK! IS HE STILL THERE?!?

TO BUSES

REMNANTS OF "HERRING McNUGGET" MEAL

DAMP KLEENEX

IT'S ALL IN ONE'S NAME, SOMEHOW...

..ONE'S DESTINY, I MEAN. EVER NOTICE HOW PEOPLE LIVE UP... OR **DOWN**...TO THE NAMES THEY'RE BORN WITH?

WOULD JOHN KENNEDY BE... **John Kennedy** ... IF HE'D BEEN BORN "MORTIMER DIPTHONG"?

WOULD FLORENCE NIGHTINGALE HAVE BEEN A HIT AS "LULU McADOO"?

ERNEST HEMINGWAY... MICK JAGGER... THOMAS JEFFERSON.... THESE PEOPLE JUST WOULDN'T HAVE MADE IT AS "BIFF TURKLE."

YEP. IT'S COSMICALLY ORDAINED. A GUY'S NAME CAN EITHER PROMOTE HIM... OR **DOOM** HIM. NO DOUBT ABOUT IT.

ME AND CASPAR WEINBERGER ARE GONNA **BEAT** THIS!!

BY POPULAR REQUEST:

The Official HANDBOOK for better COMIX COMPREHENSION

A COMPANION GUIDE TO THE GRAPHIC IDIOSYNCRASIES OF THE MODERN COMIC PAGE... AS ILLUSTRATED IN THE FOLLOWING COMIC SCENARIO PERFORMED BY MR. M. BLOOM AND MR. OPUS:

I GOT AN IDEA!

WHAT?!

"BULBLE" [TRAD.] -SUDDEN INSPIRATION

"SURPRISLES" -SUDDEN MENTAL EXCITEMENT. POPULARIZED IN "MUTT AND JEFF," 1927-1939

"SWIVLES" -MOVEMENT, CHANGE IN DIRECTION. see "moovles"

DON'T PUSH

NUCLEAR EXPLOSIVE

LET'S BLOW YOU INTO ORBIT!

HOLY MACKEREL!!

"MOOVLES" -MOVEMENT, PHYSICAL ACTION.

DON'T PUSH

NUCLEAR EXPLOSIVE

"SWEATLES" -ANXIETY, WORRY... ORIG. SEEN IN "POPEYE," 1929. MODERN USAGE RARE. STILL OCCAS. SEEN FLYING FROM HEADS OF CHARLIE BROWN, SLUGGO AND RONALD REAGAN

CLIP 'N' SAVE

"ZIPPLES" -ACCELERATION. BASICALLY A LINEAR "MOOVLE"

ZIP!!

KABLAM!!

ZOOM!

"COMIC LICENSE" -HUMOROUS EXAGGER-ATION. FOR INSTANCE, A PENGUIN COULD NOT ACTUALLY SURVIVE THE LACK OF OXYGEN AFTER BEING BLOWN INTO THE STRATOSPHERE BY A NUCLEAR EXPLOSION.

"POOFLES" -SEVERE IMPACT. OFTEN IN ASSOC. WITH "STARS"

SHOOP!!

WHAM!

"SHOOPLES" -REVERSE "ZIPPLES"

"STARS" -SEVERE PAIN

THAT WAS GREAT!!

"BOOZLES" -INTOXICATION. IN THIS CASE, "ROOT BOOZLES"

"CRANIAL SMOKE" -BURNING HUMILIATION. CARCINOGENIC IF INHALED

AS CAN BE SEEN, WITHOUT PROPER FAMILIARITY WITH THE GRAPHIC SYMBOLS, A COMIC SEQUENCE SUCH AS THIS WOULD MAKE NO SENSE WHATSOEVER. LORD KNOWS, WE DON'T WANT THAT.

CLIP 'N' SAVE

AS A WEIRD BLOOM COUNTY SUMMER WINDS DOWN, YOUNG LADS WALLOW IN THE BLESSED WATERS OF NORMALCY...

LEAP!

..WHILE OTHERS DABBLE IN THE NORMALCY OF A HOBBY...FOR INSTANCE, A NEW HAM RADIO...

PARIS ?... COME IN, PARIS...

Earth Station WBBM 640

HELLO ? MOSCOW ? SANTIAGO ? HEL-LOOOO ?

MEANWHILE, SINISTER ALIEN FORCES GATHER TO WREAK STILL MORE WEIRDNESS UPON THE SCENE...

DENVER ?

ZYGORT DEATH SHIP

CONTINUED !

THIS IS WBBM 640... CINCINNATI ? IS THAT YOU, CINCINNATI ..?

Earth Station WBBM 640

NEGATIVE. THIS IS A ZYGORTHIAN HARVEST SHIP ORBITING 100 MILES ABOVE YOUR TRANSMITTER... ANSWER THE FOLLOWING QUERIES IMMEDIATELY:

ZYGORT DEATH SHIP

ARE EARTHLINGS WHITE OR DARK MEAT ?

Earth Station WBBM 640

CINCINNATI, RACIAL EPITHETS ARE A VIOLATION OF FCC REGULA--

AND IS RED OR WHITE WINE APPROPRIATE FOR THE MEAL ?

Earth Station WBBM 640

YOU MEAN...THIS ISN'T CINCINNATI ?... I'VE MADE ACTUAL CONTACT WITH... ALIEN INTELLIGENCE ?

MORE PRECISELY, WE ARE ZYGORTHIAN RAIDERS FROM THE BLACK NEBULA ...

HEIGHT: 1/2 MILE

ZYGORT DEATH SHIP

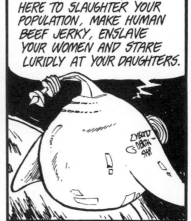

SPEAKING FRANKLY, WE'RE HERE TO SLAUGHTER YOUR POPULATION, MAKE HUMAN BEEF JERKY, ENSLAVE YOUR WOMEN AND STARE LURIDLY AT YOUR DAUGHTERS.

ZYGORT DEATH SHIP

E...EXCUSE ME... I'M FLUSH WITH THE HEADY EXHILARATION OF SCIENTIFIC TRIUMPH.

TAKE FIVE.

Earth Station WBBM 640

35

ALIENS, EH? DEATH RAYS, EH? COME TO EAT EARTHLINGS, EH? SORRY, OLIVER, BUT THIS NEWSMAN REMAINS A CHRONIC SKEPTIC...

Ooo...

LOOK. AN APPETIZER.

SHWAKK!!

HOLD... I SAY HOLD THOSE PRESSES!

SHKKKKKK

WHATCHA WANT, INTERN BLOOM?

THINK I GOT A STORY, BOSS.

AN ALIEN RAIDING SHIP HAS BEEN LASER-BLASTING MOST OF TOWN TODAY. THE SVENSON BROTHERS WERE TURNED INTO BACON. MRS. DITBURG WAS SUCKED UP INTO THE SHIP FOR PURPOSES TOO TERRIBLE TO MENTION.

I SUPPOSE YOU EXPECT ME TO BUMP MY JACK KEMP ADULTERY RUMOR STORY TO PAGE TWO!?

I DIDN'T SAY THAT!

Bloom Picayune

ZYGORTHIAN RAIDERS ATTACK FROM SPACE

KILL, MAIM, TERRORIZE... WHO ARE THESE MONSTERS? WHAT CAN BE DONE?!

THIS IS ALL ILLEGAL... JUST PLAIN ILLEGAL... YOU WANNA KNOW WHAT NEEDS TO BE DONE?...

SHKKKWAK!!

BY GOSH, A SPECIAL CONGRESSIONAL INVESTIGATING COMMITTEE NEEDS TO GET TO THE BOTTOM OF THIS!!

PUGH.

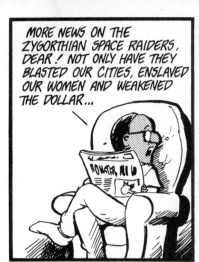

NOW, MR. ALIEN MONSTER... ON JULY 23RD, YOU DESTROYED DETROIT, YOU BLEW UP 736 WORKS OF ABSTRACT PUBLIC SCULPTURE... AND YOU TURNED JOAN COLLINS AND PETER HOLM INTO CABBAGE... NOW... ER...

SIR... WHAT *IS* THAT ALL OVER YOUR TABLE?

TELEGRAMS OF SUPPORT.

I QUIT.

RIDLEY, SIT *DOWN,* YOU YELLOW SPUD!

SHOCKED! YES, SHOCKED I AM AT THE TREAT-MENT OF THIS HEROIC WITNESS...

WELL, THERE HE GOES! SO HE BROKE A FEW RULES... THE GALAXY COULD USE A FEW MORE "TAKE-CHARGE"-TYPE ALIEN MARAUDERS LIKE HIM!

CAUTION SLAVES ON BOARD

BUT I HAVE THIS TERRIBLE VISION OF HIM IN HIS SPACESHIP... SAFELY AWAY FROM GULLIBLE EARTHLING EYES..

...HE STRIPS OFF HIS CHARISMATIC, CUDDLY, "CAN-DO"-KINDA-GUY DISGUISE, REVEALING HIS TRUE, HORRIBLE, BEADY-EYED SHAPE...

WHAT'S HE LOOK LIKE??

ADMIRAL POINDEXTER.

HANG HIM!

MY WHOLE LIFE HAS BEEN ONE LONG EXERCISE IN THE AVOIDANCE OF CONFLICT.

OH, IT HAS NOT.

IT HAS.

THAT'S RIDICULOUS.

IF THAT'S RIDICULOUS, THEN *I'M* RIDICULOUS.

YOU'RE NOT RIDICULOUS.

TELL ME WHAT WE'RE ARGUING ABOUT.

HAVEN'T THE FAINTEST.

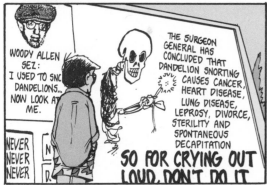

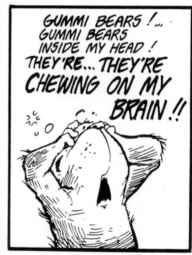

40

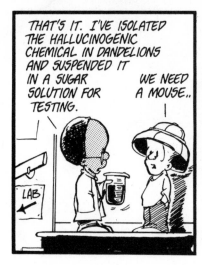
THAT'S IT. I'VE ISOLATED THE HALLUCINOGENIC CHEMICAL IN DANDELIONS AND SUSPENDED IT IN A SUGAR SOLUTION FOR TESTING.

WE NEED A MOUSE...

LAB

FREEZE, SON. YOU'VE GOT JUST WHAT I WANT.

GULP! GULP! GULP! GULP!

I BETTER GO HIDE PAPA MOUSE'S GUNS.

WASN'T THIS A "LUCY" EPISODE?

HONEY...PLEASE COME OUT OF THE TOOL SHED...

OLIVER SAYS YOU MIGHT BE FEELING A TEENSY BIT FUNNY AFTER ACCIDENTALLY DRINKING SOME DANDELION EXTRACT...

Chef

DEAR?

NOW WHAT?

ELEANOR...CALL 911. ERIK ESTRADA IS TRYING TO COME OUT OF MY NAVEL!

Chef

OH, GEORGE...COME BACK TO US! ERIK ESTRADA IS **NOT** IN YOUR STOMACH...

YES HE IS! OH, IT HURTS!

GEORGE...YOU HAVE TO ASK YOURSELF HOW MR. ESTRADA COULD HAVE GOTTEN INTO YOUR TUMMY IN THE FIRST PLACE...

THEN YOU HAVE TO ASK YOURSELF... WHY ERIK ESTRADA? IT COULD JUST AS EASILY BE JAMES BROLIN...

Chef

HAVE YOU ASKED YOURSELF THAT, GEORGE?

NO. WHY DON'T YOU ASK **HIM**, ELEANOR?

41

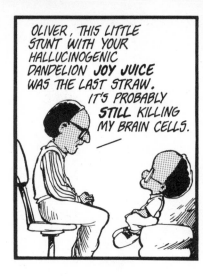

OLIVER, THIS LITTLE STUNT WITH YOUR HALLUCINOGENIC DANDELION **JOY JUICE** WAS THE LAST STRAW. IT'S PROBABLY **STILL** KILLING MY BRAIN CELLS.

SO HELP ME, IT'S TIMES LIKE THIS I WISH I JUST HAD A DITZY-HEADED DAUGHTER WHO WOULDN'T KNOW A TEST TUBE IF IT WALKED UP AND BIT HER ON THE LEG.

HOLD IT.

WHY DO YOU LOOK LIKE A BIG XEROX OF BROOKE SHIELDS?

FLASHBACK, DAD. JUST SAVOR THE IRONY.

GOOD MORNING AND HAPPY BIRTHDAY, DAD.

MY INTERNAL BODY PARTS ARE 40 YEARS OLD.

...47 DELICATE, FRAGILE ORGANS...ALL PUMPING, CRANKING, WHIRRING ALONG WITHOUT A GLITCH FOR 40 YEARS...

MY GOD...MY CAR WON'T RUN FOR TWO MONTHS WITHOUT SOMETHING BUSTING. HOW LONG CAN MY LUCK HOLD OUT??

AW, COME **ON**, DA—

DON'T JOSTLE THE BED!!

47 FRAGILE ORGANS... 200 MILES OF DELICATE BLOOD VESSELS... 12 MILLION COMPLEX-CHEMICAL REACTIONS TO CORRECTLY HAPPEN EVERY SECOND...

EVEN IF I **CAN** KEEP IT ALL FROM BURSTING, BREAKING, SPLITTING, SPURTING OR CORRODING ... I'LL JUST... I'LL...

YOU KNOW.

..GET HIT BY A BUS, FALL ON A DIRTY SOUP SPOON AND CATCH AIDS?

YOU UNDERSTAND.

OKAY. RIGHT. YES. YOU **ARE** 40 YEARS OLD TODAY.

AND YES...THE HUMAN BODY IS UNFATHOMABLY DELICATE IN ITS AWESOME COMPLEXITY... BUT I JUST DON'T SEE WHAT THOSE TWO FACTS HAVE TO DO WITH EACH OTHER.

KLUNK

DON'T LET IT SHAKE YA, POP... **HANG** IN THERE !!

≋SIGH≋

LET'S START YOUR BIRTHDAY OVER AGAIN, DAD.

NOW. LET'S JUST LOOK AT FORTY AS A TIME FOR A **RENEWAL OF PERSPECTIVE** ...

LOOK AT THE WORLD AS IF IT'S BRAND NEW ! SEE THINGS AS IF YOU'VE NEVER SEEN THEM BEFORE !

STARTLING, EH ?

YOU LOOK LIKE BUCKWHEAT.

I.. I WANT TO GROW UP... AND BRING DOWN DUMB MEN IN HIGH POSITIONS !

I WANT TO BECOME A GAME-SHOW HOSTESS AND EARN MILLIONS ! I WANT TO STAR IN A JAMES BOND MOVIE ! OR A ROCK VIDEO ! OR BE A PROFESSIONAL CHEERLEADER !

THE OPPORTUNITIES ARE INFINITE !! I MIGHT EVEN BE ... MISS AMERICA ! YES, I WANT TO GROW UP TO BE...

...A BIMBO.

YA GOTTA CHASE YER DREAMS, BABY.

MEANWHILE, AT THE PLUSH, MODERN OFFICES OF THE TIGHTLY COMPETITIVE "BLOOM PICAYUNE"...

C'MON, BOSS.

NO. GOD, NO.

CONSIDER THE MARKET, BOSS.

NO NO NO NO NO NO NO NO NO...

AWRIGHT! PUT CHRISTIE BRINKLEY ON PAGE ONE AND RUN THE WEATHER MAP ACROSS SIX PAGES IN 93 EYE-CATCHING COLORS!! AWRIGHT! AWRIGHT!!

THE DREADED "USA TODAY" EFFECT.

≥ CLICK ≥

THE TOP MUCKY-MUCKS OF THE "BLOOM PICAYUNE" ARE HAVING AN EXECUTIVE MEETING.

..NO DOUBT DISCUSSING THE SAME THINGS BEING DISCUSSED IN MEDIA BOARDROOMS ALL AROUND THE COUNTRY...

GENTLEMEN..OUR SECULAR-HUMANIST, WEALTH-DISTRIBUTING, INSTITUTION-WRECKING AGENDA IS ON SCHEDULE. EXCEL-LENT. I'LL NOTIFY MOSCOW.

BOY, DIDN'T YA ALWAYS KINDA SUSPECT AS MUCH?

DID YA GET ME "PISTACHIO NUT" LIKE I TOLD YA?

STEVE... I HAVE AN IMPROVEMENT OVER ICE CREAM...

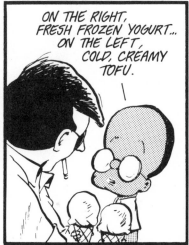
ON THE RIGHT, FRESH FROZEN YOGURT... ON THE LEFT, COLD, CREAMY TOFU.

I HAVE SEEN THE FUTURE OF FROZEN DESSERT... AND IT IS YEAST CULTURE AND BEAN CURD.

KICKING AND SCREAMING WILL THE FOOLISH BE DRAGGED INTO THE 21ST CENTURY.

OLIVER! DON'T LEAVE US TO YOUR PAST! THE MODERN WORLD IS SHINY... BUT IT'S ALSO **COLD**! HERE... SAY HELLO TO SOMEONE YOU HAVEN'T SEEN FOR A WHILE...

YOU CAN COME OUT NOW...

GOOD **HEAVENS**... IT'S... IT'S...

..MY OLD SLIDE RULE.

YOU'VE SEEMED SO... DISTANT LATELY.

SO... HOW'VE YA BEEN?

AWFUL. YOU DON'T CALL. YOU DON'T WRITE... WHAT'S A SLIDE RULE SUPPOSED TO THINK?

WE HAD SOME LAUGHS... BUT... TIMES ARE DIFFERENT.

THERE'S SOMEBODY ELSE... I CAN TELL. WHO IS IT? **TEXAS INSTRUMENTS**?

OF COURSE. YOUNGER... SEXIER... WITH A COUPLE OF BIG GAZONGA **MICROCHIPS**, I BET...

MAYBE.

ALL SILICON. THEY'LL BE SHOT BY FORTY. WATCH.

SADLY, OLIVER BADE HIS RAGGED OL' TEDDY AND WORN-OUT SLIDE RULE GOODBYE AS THEY RELUCTANTLY RETURNED TO HIS MEMORIES.

THEY WERE RIGHT, OF COURSE. THE THINGS FROM OUR PAST ARE SOMEHOW THE DEAREST...

..AND AS HE SNUGGLED BACK INTO BED, OLIVER TUCKED IN WITH HIM ONE VERY SPECIAL THOUGHT GLEANED FROM THIS PHANTOM EVENING:

IF ANYONE EVER TOOK HIS "RAMBO NAPALM RIFLE" AWAY FROM HIM, HE'D JUST DIE.

49

50

I'M SO HAPPY. I'M DRIVING TO VEGAS WITH THE BANJO PLAYER FROM "DELIVERANCE" AND HIS PET SLEDGE-HAMMER.

WHAT THIS SCRIPT NEEDS IS A QUICK *REWRITE*...

ERASE ERASE ERASE... SCRIBBLE SCRIBBLE SCRIBBLE...

NOW WE'RE COOKIN'!

ZSA ZSA GABOR CIRCA 1963

GOODBYE! THANKS FOR THE LIFT, ZSA ZSA! SAY HELLO TO EVA FOR ME!

VROOOM!

NOW, THIS IS WHAT'S GOING ON: ZSA ZSA HAS DROPPED ME HERE AT CAESAR'S PALACE. NEXT I'LL GO UP TO THE SINATRA SUITE FOR A 'SCHNOZZ' MASSAGE BY JULIE ANDREWS.

SEZ IT ALL RIGHT HERE IN THE...ER...

WHERE'S THE SCRIPT? THIS ISN'T VEGAS... *WHERE'S THE SCRIPT?*

BACK IN THE CAR.

VIRTUALLY *SCRIPTLESS*, OUR PROTAGONIST WANDERS THE WILDERNESS OF THE AMERICAN LANDSCAPE...

GASP... GASP..

NO STORY...NO DIALOGUE... NO ISSUES...NO THEMES...

WATER...

HE'S *COMPLETELY* WITHOUT DIRECTION...

AUGH..

HE IS NOT, HOWEVER, WITHOUT HIS NEEDLE-SHARP INSTINCTS FOR A SNAPPY METAPHOR..

BOY! I FEEL LIKE THE DEMOCRATIC PARTY!

FIRST OFFICER SPOCK BACK FROM SHORE LEAVE AND REPORTING FOR DUTY!

STAR BASE ALPHA BLOOM

SULU, MY MAN!

YOU'VE BEEN REPLACED. WE HAVE A NEW MISTER SPOCK WITH A NEW PERSPECTIVE ON THE CHARACTER.

A NEW SPOCK?!

AT THE MOMENT HE'S HAVING A TYPICAL DISAGREEMENT WITH DR. McCOY...

BONES, I HATE YOUR ☆§!%#⚡@ HUMAN GUTS. DISCUSSION?

NO.

SULU, FETCH ME A MARTINI.

VULCANS DON'T DRINK BOOZE.

OR SAY "FETCH".

I'M A "NOUVEAU-VULCAN" AND I'M TAKING OVER THE SHIP. WE'RE NOW ON A FIVE-YEAR MISSION FOR CHEAP PLEASURES.

SACRILEGE!

WHATTA WE DO?

HUMOR HIM. I'LL SEND OUT A DISCREET DISTRESS CODE...

SULU..BEAM UP SEVERAL DRUNK SORORITY GIRLS WITH SMALL NOSES.

UH--

GOD HELP US!!

SIGH...

SPOCK #1!! YOU'RE REHIRED!

SPOCK #2 HAS GONE INTO VULCAN HORMONAL IMBALANCE! HE'S SCREAMING FOR A SLAVE HAREM OF SUPPLE PASSION DROIDS!! HE'S BERSERK!

RUN!

I'LL JUST SET THE OL' PHASER ON "EMASCULATE".

TOO SMALL

THE BLOOM COUNTY CHARACTER ASSASSINATIONAL ASSOCIATION IS **ON STRIKE** FOR A NEW, **LARGER** COMIC-STRIP **SIZE STANDARD** TO AVOID LEGIBILITY PROBLEMS JUST SUCH AS THIS EXACT ONE.

CHIRP!

GONE ON STRIKE

BLACK SCIENTIST TODAY

KEEP YER SHORTS ON... I'M A-MOVIN' JEST AS LICKETY DAMN SPLIT AS AH CAN...

ROSEBUD ESQ.

UNION

I'M W.A. THORNHUMP, CEO OF BLOOM COUNTY PRODUCTIONS, INC. ...HERE TO DISCUSS AN UGLY RESULT OF OUR CURRENT LABOR TROUBLES...

GRAPHIC VANDALISM!

PROFITS

STRIKE

BLOOM COUNTY, INC.
"Your Best Comic Value"

UNION THUGS VANDALIZED YESTERDAY'S SUNDAY RERUN COMIC BY SCRAWLING AN ANTI-MANAGEMENT OBSCENITY WITHIN THE ARTWORK. TO THESE INK-WIELDING TERRORISTS, THERE CAN BE BUT **ONE** RESPONSE:

HEIGHTENED VIGILANCE AGAINST FURTHER ATTACKS!

Recently had Liposuction To Buttocks

BLOOM COUNTY CHAIRMAN W.A. THORNHUMP HERE... JUST AN "ANGEL OF EQUITY" OVERSEEING EVENTS DURING THIS TROUBLED TIME OF LABOR RESTLESSNESS...

YET THERE ARE THOSE WHO WOULD ACCUSE ME...ME!... OF THE UNFAIR USE OF THIS MEDIUM FOR PROPAGANDA PURPOSES...

THERE IS BUT ONE WAY TO RESPOND TO THESE GANGSTERS AND PHILISTINES...

BLOOM COUNTY, INC. "Your Best Comic Value"

The Evil Connection

KHADAFY → COMMIES
↓ UNIONS ↓
SIN → HEMORRHOIDS

STRIKE

BLOOM COUNTY, INC. "Your Best Comic Value"

In the absence of the striking union characters, Bloom County management officials will be temporarily providing the day's waggish entertainment.

Today: Mr. Will J. Knudson, Asst. Director of Accounting

AHEM. LOVE IS THE PLEASANT INTERVAL BETWEEN MEETING A BEAUTIFUL GIRL AND DISCOVERING SHE LOOKS LIKE A HADDOCK.

HEE HEE HEE HEE HEE

BILL THE CAT: UNGH.

UNION 1, MANAGEMENT 0.

Today: Ms. Leona O'Connor, Exec. Vice President of Bloom County, Inc. will tell a funny political joke.

All of us here in management are behind you the whole way, Leona! Go for it, girl!

BILL CASEY WALKED UP TO THE GATES OF HEAVEN AND SAID TO ANGEL GABRED---GABRIEL... ST. GABRIEL... PETER GABRIEL... NO NO...

OH FORGET THIS, W.A.... JUST SETTLE WITH THE STRIKERS.

THAT'S FUNNY, LEONA! YOU'RE FIRED.

Y-Y-YA SAID THERE W-WAS ABOUT S-S-SSSSSEVENTY MILLION PEOPLE READIN' THIS THING?

AAAIGH!

New Marketing Director Ned "Crack 'em Up" Katston was going to tell the story about the priest, the rabbi and the girdle salesman, but he has apparently choked in the clutch.

Ned soon will be moving back to shipping, where, he should be happy to learn, his audience will be about two.

..THOSE CRUMMY, UNGRATEFUL EMPLOYEES... THE STRIP'S PROFITS PLUMMETING... THE PUBLIC'S LOYALTY DRIFTING AWAY LIKE FALL LEAVES...

WHAT'S TO BE DONE?

OF COURSE! A DOUBLE WHAMMY! TOMORROW I GO ON WITH AN IACOCCA APPLE-PIE, ALL-AMERICAN PITCH...

AND NEXT WEEK... HIRE PERMANE-- ER... TEMPORARY CHARACTERS... HEE HEE

SCABS?!

STRIKE HDQS.

The Bloom Picayune

STRIKE TENSIONS NEAR HYSTERIA

RANK AND FILE GROWS RESTLESS... UGLY VIOLENCE FEARED LIKELY AS DEFECTING UNION CHARACTERS CROSS PICKET LINES

THORNHUMP: "I LUV STRIKES"

STOPPIT! LEMME THRU! GET BACK, YOU LEFTIST MOB OF KENNEDYESQUE RABBLE-ROUSERS!!

LOOK...I'M SORRY, BUT I SIMPLY NEED MY PAYCHEC--.

SPLAT!

I JUST DON'T KNOW MYSELF ANYMORE...

PRINT COMIX BIGGER

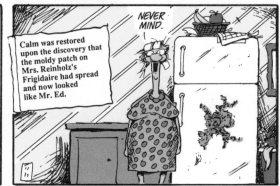

I GOT A SCENE WITH OPUS! DID **SOMEBODY** REMEMBER TO HIRE HIS SCAB REPLACEMENT?!!

'ELLO, MATE!

LI'L OLLIE FUNT 'ERE... BLOODY WELL EXCITED 'BOUT A NEW CAREER! SO LET'S GET DOWN TO **SOME SERIOUS** ☆%$#!! @#%* **BUSINESS!!**

FINE..HERE'S THE SCENE: "STEVE IS ON THE FLOOR. A JEALOUS GIRLFRIEND HAS JUST CUT HIS LEGS OFF WITH A CARROT PEELER..."

YEAH.. OKAY.. I'VE GOT THE NUANCES...

"..THEN OPUS WALKS IN AND SAYS SOMETHING WISTFULLY POIGNANT."

"REAGAN SUCKS!"

FIRED?

I'M SORRY, MR. FUNT... YOU'RE JUST FAR TOO URBANE FOR US HERE ON THE COMIX PAGE...

Bloom County, Inc.

WELL, YA GOT **THAT ONE** RIGHT, MATE... GEEZ, WHAT A BUNCH O' RUBES... **I'M OUTTA HERE!**

OPUS DEODORANT STICKS

OPUS ACNE CREAM

OPUS GUM

OPUS AIR FRESHENER

OPUS CEREAL

KITTY SALT

OPUS MUG

OPUS ASPARAGUS STRAINER

≈SNIFF!≈ SOMEDAY...

Bloom Picayune

IT'S OVER!

UNION CAVES... RANK AND FILE RETURNS... MANAGEMENT HOLDS FIRM ON MAINTAINING MINIATURE SIZE OF NEWSPAPER COMICS...

"HEE HEE HEE HEE HEE HEE!"

FAILURE... DEFEAT... LIFE PERMANENTLY STALLED AT PRESHRUNK PROPORTIONS...

DIDN'T THEY THROW US **ANY** CONCESSIONARY BONES?

STRIKE

MELANCHODY LION PATCH

WELL, THORNHUMP DID PROMISE "GOOD-FAITH EFFORTS TO IMPROVE READABILITY AT THIS SIZE."

MEANING WHAT?

STRIKE

MELANCHOLY LION PATCH

DUNNO.

GOSH...

MELAN-PATCH

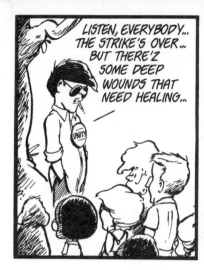

69

LET'S JUST GET TO THE FACTS: DURING TEATIME ON A RECENT BLUSTERY SUNDAY, A STRONG GUST CAUGHT A LOCAL BASSELOPE'S EARS, AND HE DID, IN FACT, BECOME AIRBORNE.

SAILING EAST, HE FOUND MRS. NUSBAUM'S LAUNDRY LINE, AND IN PARTICULAR, SHORTS BELONGING TO MR. NUSBAUM, WHO LATER BLAMED THEIR DISAPPEARANCE ON SOCIALISTS.

SHUUMP!

AT 4:16 P.M., A NEAR MISS WITH A UFO WAS REPORTED BY DELTA AIRLINES, WHICH WAS HAVING A BAD YEAR ANYWAY.

5:01 P.M. PINKERTON AIR FORCE BASE FIRED A GROUND-TO-AIR HEAT-SEEKING MISSILE AT A SUSPECTED IRANIAN SUICIDE PARATROOPER WEARING BOXER SHORTS. IT MISSED.

ZING!

SHKKKK!!

BLAM!

BY 6 P.M., THE MEADOW CRISIS TEAM HAD MOBILIZED AND DID EVENTUALLY BRING THE SITUATION UNDER CONTROL. WITH SOME DIFFICULTY.

THE FAA PROMISED A FULL INVESTIGATION. NEVERTHELESS, THERE WAS SOME IRRESPONSIBLE AND PREMATURE SPECULATION REGARDING THE EXACT CAUSE OF THE AFTERNOON'S UNFORTUNATE EVENTS.

FORGET TO SAY OUR PRAYERS, DID WE?

I SAY... YOU **ARE** A *WILD Animal*, AREN'T YOU?

YEP.

EXCUSE ME, BUT HAVE YOU EVER BEEN TRAPPED, SHOT, POISONED, PIERCED, NETTED, CLUBBED, HOOKED, PICKLED, BLUDGEONED, BEATEN, BATTERED OR BEHEADED?

NOPE.

EVER BEEN SKINNED, SMOKED, STUFFED, GUTTED, FRIED, FILETED, BASTED, BROILED, BARBECUED, ROASTED OR TOASTED?

NOPE.

... CAUGHT, CAGED, TESTED, DISPLAYED, TRAINED, REINED, MAIMED, INJECTED, INFECTED, REJECTED, TORMENTED OR TORTURED?

NOPE.

YOU JUST RUN AROUND ALL DAY DOIN' **NOTHIN'**?

YEP.

HERE'S ONE!

SWISH! PHOOM! BLAM! BLAM! BLAM! WOOOSH! BLAM! SNAP!

MY **GOD**, IT SEEMED SO **REAL**!!

THE STOCK MARKET... IT CRASHED! OUR BLUE-CHIP STOCKS CRUMBLED!... ALONG WITH MY HOPES TO BUY A NEW BOAT THIS SUMMER!!

WHEW! IT **WAS** ALL JUST A HORRIBLE NIGHTMARE, WASN'T IT? OF COURSE IT WAS. CAN I HAVE SOME WARM MILK?

4:20 a.m. IS NO TIME FOR HONESTY.

LEAVE THE LIGHT ON. OKAY?

IT'S BEEN THREE WEEKS, DAD. TIME TO FACE THE POST-WALL-STREET-CRASH REALITIES.

AS OF OCT. 1ST, OUR BROKER SAYS OUR NET WORTH IS ABOUT SIX DOLLARS.

NOW... FOR INSTANCE... HOW MIGHT THIS BIT OF NEWS AFFECT OUR PLANS TO BUY A NEW BOAT THIS SUMMER?

MY GOD. WE'RE GOING TO HAVE TO SETTLE FOR THE MORE FUEL-EFFICIENT 260 h.p. 350 MAGS IN THAT BABY...

LET'S START OVER.

TO HECK WITH OUR #73,400 LOSS ON THE STOCK MARKET! OUR LIFESTYLE IS NOT CHANGING!

YOU'RE GOING TO HARVARD... WE'RE RE-PAINTING THE BATHROOM, AND I **WILL** BUY THAT 41-FOOT "MIAMI VICE" SPEEDBOAT!!

RRRING!

YES, WE MAY BE A LITTLE SHORT IN LIQUID ASSETS, BUT I WILL NOT RUN A DEFICIT IN ONE AREA:

MY PRIDE!!

PAT! PAT! PAT!

WE PASSED THE HAT! I CONTRIBUTED TWO STALE "ZINGERS"!

CHIN UP!

THURSDAYS ARE SLOW NEWS DAYS HERE AT THE INTERNATIONAL "BLOOM PICAYUNE."

AT TIMES LIKE THIS WE LIKE TO SIT AROUND AND FANTASIZE ABOUT THE ULTIMATE DREAM HEADLINE...

"SUPREME COURT NOMINEE... FOUND TO HAVE SOLD ARMS TO KURT WALDHEIM... DURING TRYST WITH PRINCESS DI... WHILE STOCK MARKET FALLS... DOWN A WELL."

"BUSH IS AHEAD BY THREE POINTS... DOLE BACK BY TWO! GORE UP FOUR!"

TAP TAP

"JACKSON'S FALTERING! ROBERTSON SEEN RUNNING TWO POINTS AHEAD OF DUKAKIS IN DUBUQUE!"

TAP TAP TAP TAP

"WITH ONLY SEVERAL HUNDRED MONTHS TO GO, IT'S GEPHARDT NECK AND NECK WITH ALF THE ALIEN IN ALBUQUERQUE!!"

THE MODERN POLITICAL REPORTER PAUSES TO REFLECT ON THE EXHAUSTIVE DEPTH OF HIS POLITICAL ANALYSIS...

BOSS!

YES, JUNIOR INTERN MILO.!!

REMEMBER ALL OUR SENSATIONAL, PANIC-CAUSING STORIES ABOUT THE GREAT CHILD-STEALING EPIDEMIC?!

YEAH?

THERE NEVER REALLY WAS ONE!

GREAT SCOTT! RUN A CORRECTION BELOW THE TIDE SCHEDULES ON PAGE 109!!

STOP THE PRESSES!

73

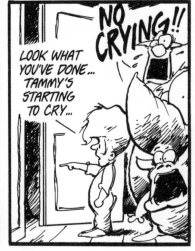

77

EXCUSE ME, MADAM... AN EMERGENCY...

OUR VEHICLE IS STUCK AND WE COULD USE A LITTLE MORE WEIGHT FOR TRACTION.

HI. NO SNOW TIRES. HOW LONG'S THIS GONNA TAKE? WE EXPECT A THAW IN APRIL.

DON'T KID ME, BUDDY. YOU DON'T NEED MY HELP. THIS THING'S FOUR-WHEEL-DRIVE. YOU'RE RIGHT. I'M A BAD BOY.

LOOK, YOU'RE VERY CUTE, BUT UNLESS THERE'S SOME OTHER WINTER CRISIS I CAN HELP THAW, I'LL BE ON MY WAY. MNG LI AH FLOZA.

WHAT? MNG LI AH FLOZA.

WHAT'S HE SAYING? FLOZA! HE SAYS HIS LIPS ARE FROZEN.

MR. SULU! THE CAPTAIN WANTS TO KNOW IF YOU'VE FOUND ANY LITHZANI-WHATCHAMACALLIT FUEL CRYSTALS? NO. LET'S GO FOR A COUPLE OF BOURBONS...

WE INTERRUPT THIS STORY TO CLEAR UP A GROWING CONTROVERSY: PORTNOY'S EXACT ANIMAL SPECIES. WE NOW GO TO PROF. J.B. DOLSON AT THE UNIV. OF TEXAS BIOLOGY DEPT.:

UNEQUIVOCALLY... THE LITTLE BEAST IS Marmota monax ... "THE COMMON GROUNDHOG."

PLEASE CONTINUE. I DON'T WORK WITH PIGS. I THOUGHT I WAS A LLAMA!!! I SWEAR!

81

HERE. IT'S A McDONALD'S GIFT CERTIFICATE FOR A "BIG MAC." MERRY CHRISTMAS.

OH, THANK YOU!

AND THIS IS FOR YOU... A MINIATURE BRONZE BUST OF MYSELF THAT I PAINSTAKINGLY CRAFTED AS A GESTURE OF OUR ETERNAL FRIENDSHIP.

YESSIR.. SIXTEEN LONG MONTHS IT TOOK...

HERE'S ANOTHER ONE FOR A LARGE FRIES!

NO, NO... WOULDN'T THINK OF IT...

OH, PORTNOY!

OH, NO...

GET AWAY FROM ME, OPUS! YOU JUST WANNA GIVE ME ONE OF YOUR ABSURDLY SPECTACULAR CHRISTMAS GIFTS, SO YOU CAN ACT SMUG ABOUT IT ALL YEAR LONG!!

I HAVE SOMETHING FOR YOU...

NO! GET AWAY!!

HERE. IT'S A SWEATER I KNITTED OUT OF TEN YEARS' WORTH OF MY BELLYBUTTON LINT.

THANKS. HERE'S YOUR YELLOWSTONE SOUVENIR ASHTRAY.

MERRY CHRISTMAS, MILO.

OH, NO, YOU DON'T...

EVERY CHRISTMAS YOU FEEL DEPRESSED ABOUT YOUR MOM, AND EVERY CHRISTMAS YOU DEAL WITH IT BY PLAYING THE MARTYR WITH YOUR AWE-INSPIRING, UNMATCHABLE GIFTS! WELL, I WON'T BE PART OF YOUR GUILT TRIP!!

HEY... C'MON... DON'T DO THAT... LOOK, I'M SORRY. I'D LOVE TO RECEIVE YOUR GIFT...

SNIFF!

AH. THE ENTIRE GREAT WALL OF CHINA PERSONALLY CARVED TO 1/1000 SCALE IN SOLID BRASS.

GOLD. MELTED DOWN MY FILLINGS.

86

NOW, BOBBY, YOUR SISTER SAYS YOU RECEIVED 37 TOYS OF DEATH AND HUMAN DESTRUCTION FOR CHRISTMAS, CORRECT?

THINK THAT'S AN APPROPRIATE WAY TO CELEBRATE JESUS' BIRTHDAY?

TURNING INTO A LITTLE WAR-GLORIFYING SOCIOPATH, AREN'T WE, BOBBY?

—BOBBY?

.YOUR WITNESS.

LAWYERS DIE.

THANK YOU, MONICA. SANTA CLAUS'S VIOLENT CHRISTMAS GIFTS TO YOUR BROTHER ARE INDEED A SAD LEGACY. YOUR WITNESS, COUNSELOR.

ISN'T IT TRUE, MISS GELP, THAT IN MARCH 1985 YOU YOURSELF SPECIFICALLY REQUESTED A POTENTIALLY LETHAL TOY WEAPON FOR CHRISTMAS?! ISN'T IT? ISN'T IT?!

NO FURTHER QUESTIONS.

IT WAS A "BARBIE" NAIL FILE.

OBJECTION!!

YOU MEAN TO SAY THAT YOU'RE ST. NICK, ALIAS "SANTA CLAUS"?

HAD TO LOSE A FEW POUNDS TO FIT INTO MY NEW SAAB.

39 MILLION TOY GUNS WERE RECEIVED THIS CHRISTMAS, MR. CLAUS...

...ON A 31% MARGIN. DARN GOOD YEAR.

WHAT HAPPENED TO THE TRUE MEANING OF CHRISTMAS, NICK?!

C'MON. IN 1987? HO! HO!

THE PLAINTIFF SMUGLY RESTS HER CASE.

HO! HO! HO! HO! HO! HO! HO! HO!

88

LADIES AND GENTLEMEN OF THE JURY... THIS LAWSUIT IS ABOUT CHRISTMAS... IT'S ABOUT WAR TOYS... IT'S ABOUT GREED AND FALLEN IDEALS...

... IT'S ABOUT GOD SENDING MY BOY TO PURGATORY IF HE SUCCEEDS IN ATTACKING SANTA CLAUS !!

ZIP!

DON'T LISTEN TO HIM. THE NUMSKULL'S BEEN LIVING ON POP-TARTS AND ISN'T THINKING CLEARLY. THIS WHOLE THING IS DISGRACEFUL. IGNORE HIM.

SEE YOU BACK AT THE HOUSE, DEAR.

MA, HAVE YOU HEARD OF THE MOVIE "THROW MOMMA FROM THE TRAIN"?

CONGRATULATIONS ON SUCCESSFULLY FIGHTING MY LAWSUIT, MR. CLAUS.

SANTA, INC.

I WAS KINDA THINKING WE'D JUST LET BYGONES BE BYGONES.

SO YOU WILL BRING MY LITTLE BROTHER, BOBBY, A PRESENT NEXT CHRISTMAS, WON'T YOU?

YEP! A REAL "CHUCK NORRIS TOY GRENADE LAUNCHER"!

I WAS THINKING OF JUST A NICE, PEACEFUL RUBBER BALL.

SORRY. THEY'RE ALL SAVED TO FILL ORDERS FROM NORTHERN IRELAND AND THE MIDEAST.

SO! DID YA WIN THE BIG COURT CASE? FOR ONCE?

SHUT UP OR I'LL STUFF LEECHES UP YOUR NOSE.

O FOR 92, IS IT?

GRRRRR...

89

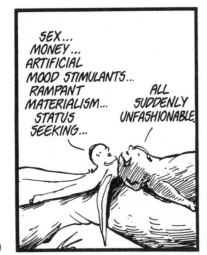

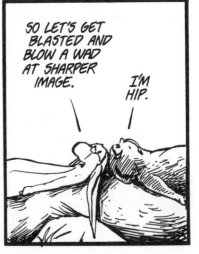

MEANWHILE...BACK AT THE MIGHTY BASTION OF JOURNALISTIC INTEGRITY...

...THE BEACON OF LIGHT IN THE DARKNESS OF IGNORANCE...

...THE STRONGHOLD OF HUMAN INSIGHT... THE BULWARK OF FREE THOUGHT! THE SWORD OF TRUTH IN MAN'S ETERNAL PURSUIT OF FREE EXPRESSION AND DEMOCRACY...

..YES... THE "DAILY BLOOM PICAYUNE"!!

THE "PERSONALS" SECTION OR THE WHOLE PAPER IN GENERAL?

RRRING!!

CITY DESK

THIS IS GARY HART! TRY FOLLOWING ME AROUND THIS TIME, SMART GUYS!

GO ON! FOLLOW ME! I DARE YOU! SEE IF YOU FIND ANYTHING, YOU SNEAKING, SKULKING, YELLOW MEDIA DOGS! HA! JUST TRY IT!

OKAY.

I'LL BE AT PANCHO'S PALACE OF PLEASURE. AROUND EIGHT.

HELLO! "PICAYUNE" PERSONALS.

HI. THIS IS GARY HART.

SAY, IF MY WIFE CALLS, TELL HER I'M...UH...IN TIBET FOR THE WEEKEND. FORGET I SAID THAT! KEEP OUT OF MY FAMILY LIFE, YOU MEDIA JACKALS!

CLICK.

RRRRING!

HELLO!

THIS IS GARY. DO YOU SUPPOSE THAT JESSICA HAHN MIGHT LIKE BIMINI? FORGET I SAID THAT! FOLLOW ME! GO ON! YOU'LL BE BORED!!

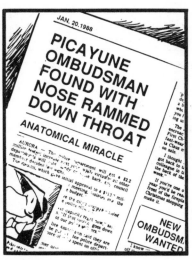

GOOD MORNING! THE RUSSIANS STILL BEATING THE PANTS OFF US IN SPACE?

247ᵗʰ SHUTTLE DELAY FAUCETS LEAK

AAIIGH.!!

AARRGGHH

BOING! BOING BOING BOING

IT APPEARS INDUBITABLY SO.

I'D LIKE TO APOLOGIZE FOR YESTERDAY'S VIOLENT OUTBURST, OPUS. IT WAS VERY UNLIKE ME...

BUT I'M AFRAID I GET EMOTIONAL WHEN I THINK OF THE WORLD'S MOST POWERFUL NATION BEING OUTPERFORMED IN SPACE BY A 19TH CENTURY SOCIETY THAT STILL ISN'T CAPABLE OF BUILDING ONE... SINGLE... DECENT...

...CLOCK RADIO!!

BUT THEY MAKE A MEAN FURRY HAT! AND VODKA! OLIVER?...

AARRGH.!!

TODAY THE USSR'S SPACE AGENCY ANNOUNCED ITS GOAL FOR 1990:

UH-OH.

..TO LAND A MANNED RESEARCH BASE ON THE POLAR ICE CAP OF MARS!

SHH! QUIET! SSHH!!

COINCIDENTALLY, NASA ANNOUNCED ITS GOALS TODAY, TOO...

OH, NO.

..TO PUSH OUT ANOTHER RCA SATELLITE CAPABLE OF BROADCASTING "ISHTAR" 24 HOURS A DAY TO PUERTO RICO.

NO!

95

I DUNNO... I THINK GORBACHEV IS A WOLF IN SHEEP'S UNDER-WEAR.

IRREGARDLESS, I'M WORRIED.

"CLOTHING."

YOU **ALWAYS** MOCK MY POLITICAL INSIGHTS, AND IT MAKES ME MAD AS A **WET HATTER**!

"IRREGARDLESS" ISN'T A WORD.

MAD AS A HEN WETTER... GOODBYE AND GOOD DAY.

"HEN."

THPPT.

FROM A POLITICAL PERSPECTIVE, BOB DOLE SIMPLY CAN'T HAVE HIS CAKE AND EAT IT, TOO.

THERE.!! A WRY POLITICAL INSIGHT AND I DIDN'T MIX MY METAPHOR! DID IT MEET YOUR APPROVAL?!

NOT REALLY. THE PHRASE IS MEANINGLESS. IF YOU HAVE YOUR CAKE, YOU CAN STILL EAT IT. IT'S A DEAD CLICHÉ.

AND THAT'S THE WHOLE KIT AND CABOOSE.

HECK, AIN'T NO SKIN OFF MY STIFF UPPER LIP.

DOUBLE NEGATIVE.

YA KNOW, THE FAR RIGHT'S DECLINING INFLUENCE OVER THE PRESIDENT REMINDS ME OF A FAVORITE METAPHOR:

"YOU CAN LEAD A YAK TO WATER BUT YOU...UH.. ER..."

"BUT YOU CAN'T TEACH AN OLD DOG TO MAKE A SILK PURSE OUT OF A PIG IN A POKE."

AAIGH!

IT WAS THAT TIME...
THAT VERY **SPECIAL** TIME
IN A DEMOCRACY...

♪ PHOOM PHOOM OO!
PHOOM PHOOM OO!...

OH IT BE **TIME** TA
GO TO **CAUCUS**
AND I BE FEELIN'
MIGHTY **RAUCOUS**...

YEAH, NO **JIVE**, LET'S
CAUCUS RAUCOUS,
I AIN'T TALKIN' 'BOUT
CARACAS...

FIRST ORDER OF BUSINESS WAS
A UNANIMOUS VOTE ON THE
COMPREHENSIVE **RAP BAN**
TREATY AND THE STICKY QUES-
TION OF VERIFICATION...

YEP! HE'S
STILL
QUIET!

HAVING PASSED THE 1988
COMPREHENSIVE **RAP BAN**
TREATY, CAUCUS BUSINESS
COULD NOW HOPEFULLY
TURN ELSEWHERE...

BANG!
BANG!

WHO THE HECK
ARE WE SUPPORTING
FOR PRESIDENT
THIS YEAR?

The 1988 Meadow Caucus

♪ IF Y'ALL **DON'T** WANT THIS
WORLD ALL MESSY,
ALL YOU **BAD** DUDES
JUST VOTE RHYME-
MASTER JESSE!

SUDDENLY, ATTENTION WAS
BACK ON THE **RAP BAN** TREATY
AND THE THORNY ISSUE OF
ENFORCEMENT.

TOSS HIM
IN THE
THORNS.

NOW, DON'T
GO RIOT...
I BE
QUIET...

THE 1988 Meadow Caucus

NOW THEN, LET US
MOVE TO THE MAJOR
ISSUES...

The 1988 Meadow Caucus

APPARENTLY THERE
HAS BEEN SOME
AGITATION REGARDING
THE LACK OF A NON-
SMOKING SECTION.

THE 1988 Meadow Caucus

MIND
IF I
SMOKE?

NO.
MIND IF I
BURP
PASTRAMI
BELCHES IN
YOUR FACE?

THPEW

BURP
BURP
BURP

PEOPLE, I FEAR OUR OPTIONS FOR A MEADOW PARTY PRESIDENTIAL CANDIDATE ARE AS UGLY AS USUAL...

PORTNOY, GIVE ME A CURRENT SCANDAL REPORT ON BILL THE CAT.

CLEAN AS A BABY'S BEHIND...

NO WOMANIZING, NO PLAGIARIZING, NO MARIJUANASIZING, NO ANTI-SEMITICIZING, AND NO STUPIDICIZING FOR AT LEAST 14 MONTHS.

HE'S BEEN KEEPIN' LOW?

TEQUILA COMA. I'LL GO PEEL HIM OFF THE BATHROOM FLOOR.

I DON'T WANT TO ELECT A COMATOSE CANDIDATE. HOW 'BOUT BRUCE BABBITT?

METHINKS YOU OVERLOOK OUR CANDIDATE'S UNIQUE APPEAL...

INSTEAD OF A PRESIDENT WHO'S ASLEEP FIGURATIVELY, WE CAN HAVE ONE PASSED OUT LITERALLY! NO WONDERING. FULL DISCLOSURE!

IT'D BE AN EXCITING NEW FRONTIER IN PRESIDENTIAL COURAGE.

SO WOULD A NAME LIKE "BABBITT."

FUNNY, THESE HUMAN PRIORITIES OF OURS...

HERE WE GATHER TO HELP SHAPE THE FUTURE OF DEMOCRACY AND THE FREE WORLD...

..YET HOW EASILY OUR OWN LITTLE CONFLICTS CAN DISTRACT OUR FOCUS.

ANYBODY GOT A LIGHT?

YO!

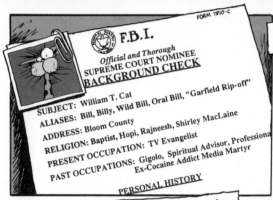

F.B.I.

Official and Thorough
SUPREME COURT NOMINEE
BACKGROUND CHECK

SUBJECT: William T. Cat

ALIASES: Bill, Billy, Wild Bill, Oral Bill, "Garfield Rip-off"

ADDRESS: Bloom County

RELIGION: Baptist, Hopi, Rajneesh, Shirley MacLaine

PRESENT OCCUPATION: TV Evangelist

PAST OCCUPATIONS: Gigolo, Spiritual Advisor, Professional Ex-Cocaine Addict Media Martyr

PERSONAL HISTORY

JUNE 10, 1972... Sucked a bong into his esophagus during a Three Dog Night concert and was forcibly ejected.

JULY, 1972... Seen on a Harvard roof with Douglas Ginsburg and Tipper Gore, smoking banana peels and arguing whether trees dream.

WOW!

MAY 3, 1986, Wash., D.C. ... Stayed up late eating watermelon with Jeane Kirkpatrick after an Anastasio Somoza Memorial Ball and spat seeds at Iranian cabbies.

MAIL

1984-1987...Repeatedly dressed up like William Casey to pull Bob Woodward's leg.

IN '83, WE TRIED TO KILL ED ASNER.

THIS IS GREAT!

LEGAL EXPERIENCE: The subject has been either convicted, indicted, jailed, under investigation or pursued by a special prosecutor for influence peddling, racketeering, obstruction of justice, perjury, shredding documents, insider trading or *Wedtech* shenanigans.

CONCLUSION: Man, don't put this loop on the bench... hire him as an administration official.

THAT IS YOUR COUNTRY! THIS IS OUR COUNTRY!

STAY OUT... WE HAVE SABERS TO RATTLE.

AND THAT IS YOUR STATE! THIS IS OUR STATE!

THANKS A LOT.

AND THAT'S YOUR TOWN! THIS IS OUR TOWN!

OUR TOWN BUG OFF

AND THIS IS OUR HOUSE! STAY OFF OUR PROPERTY!

NO TRESPASSING, BUCKAROO... WE HAVE GUNS.

EXCUSE ME. YOU'RE IN MY ROOM.

WHAT ARE YOU ALL DOING?

CIVILIZING THINGS.

YOUR ROOM?!

NOW YOU'RE IN MY PERSONAL SPACE.

IT'S BEEN A FUN WEEKEND, AND I SAY IT'S ABOUT TIME WE OFFICIALLY MET OUR SCANDAL-FREE, ELECTABLE CANDIDATE!

RAUCOUS CAUCUS '88

UH...ANYBODY KNOW WHERE OL' BILL THE CANDIDATE CAT IS?

RAUCOUS CAUCUS '88

WHISPER PSST PSST

RAUCOUS CAUCUS '88

HE'S IN AN L.A. PENTHOUSE WITH JEANE KIRKPATRICK, PLAYING "CATCH THE PERSIMMON."

GONNA BE A WHALE OF A CAMPAIGN!

RAUCOUS CAUCUS '88

OVER HERE, MISTER CAUCUS BOSS!

COULD YOU GIVE OUR CANDIDATE SOME GUIDELINES AS TO WHAT SORT OF BEHAVIOR IS POLITICAL SUICIDE FOR A PUBLIC FIGURE?

ADULTERY...LIKE HART'S. PLAGIARISM...LIKE BIDEN'S. RACIAL INSULTS...LIKE JIMMY THE GREEK'S. MIXING IN RELIGION...LIKE ROBERTSON. CRYING... LIKE PAT SCHROEDER.

RAUCOUS CAUCUS '88

HOW 'BOUT CALLING NEW YORK "HYMIETOWN" AND COZYING UP TO LOUIS FARRAKHAN?

OH, THAT'S COOL.

THE VOTES WERE VOTED. POLLS WERE POLLED. IT WAS OVER...

GOOD CAUCUS, PORT...WAS IT GOOD FOR YOU, TOO?

POLITICS: THE GREAT INTOXICANT!

SEE YOU IN '92!!

EVEN AFTER THE EXCITEMENT DIES DOWN, IT LEAVES A LINGERING BUBBLE OF NATIONALISTIC EFFERVESCENCE WITHIN THE BELLIES OF THE FAITHFUL...

SMACK SMACK

..WHICH CAN BE REMEDIED WITH PRUNES AND COD-LIVER OIL.

MUNCH MUNCH

DO YOU REALIZE THEY'VE GOT PHOTO SATELLITES UP THERE THAT CAN SEE THE COLOR OF OUR EYES...

NO DOUBT A DISTURBING REVELATION TO ALL THOSE CLANDESTINE CRIME COMMITTERS.

...NOT TO MENTION US SURREPTITIOUS NOSE PICKERS.

OLIVER TOLD ME. THEY HAVE SATELLITES THAT CAN SEE US. ANYTIME. DOING THINGS IN PRIVATE.

WHAT THINGS?

PRIVATE THINGS! YOU KNOW!

LIKE WHAT?

OH, YOU KNOW...THOSE UGLY LITTLE MINOR THINGS WE ALL DO.... BUT NOT IN FRONT OF EACH OTHER...GROSS THINGS WE NEVER IMAGINE CHRISTIE BRINKLEY DOING BUT THAT SHE PROBABLY DOES...

OH, YOU KNOW...

I'M TO UNDERSTAND YOU DO THESE THINGS?

THEY'RE WATCHING FROM ABOVE!! PRIVACY IS HISTORY! DOES ANYBODY CARE? WHERE WILL IT LEAD?!

HELLO?

SIGH...

SCRATCH SCRATCH

AND NOW FOR A SPECIAL PEEK BEHIND THE SC...

REMEMBER THIS AMAZING SCENE OF ROSEBUD FLOATING IN FRONT OF A HURTLING AIRLINER A FEW MONTHS BACK? STARTLING, ISN'T IT? FOLLOW ME AS WE REVEAL THE MAGIC WORLD WHERE THE IMPOSSIBLE BECOMES POSSIBLE: SPECIAL EFFECTS!

WOW!

FIRST STOP: THE BLOOM COUNTY MAT-PAINTING DEPT. CAROLEEN GREEN HERE IS WORKING ON ONLY ONE OF THE MANY INTRICATE SCENES YOU'VE SEEN IN THIS FEATURE THAT ARE, IN REALITY, ONLY OIL PAINT ON GLASS!

MAYBE A SMIDGEN MORE BURNT UMBER..

AND THAT HURTLING AIRLINER? MERELY A CLEVER MINIATURE FROM OUR AMAZING MODEL DEPT.!

WHOA... CHILL OUT, LORNE...

RRRROWRRR!! RAT-A-TAT-TAT BOOM!

YODA LIVES

FINALLY, THE LIVE ACTOR IS COMBINED WITH THE OTHER ELEMENTS IN OUR OPTICAL-COMPOSITING DEPT. ...AND AN EERILY REALISTIC COMIC-PAGE ILLUSION IS BORN!!

CAN YOU... YA KNOW... PROJECT A LITTLE?

AND THAT EXPLAINS HOW THE IMPOSSIBLE BECOMES POSSIBLE..

..LIKE GARY HART TAKING IOWA TOMORROW..

SPECIAL DEFECTS!

GOOD EVENING, MONSIEUR... A TABLE FOR ONE, PLEASE.

HASH 4.98

Stew 98¢

Zeke's Slop Stop

SMOKING OR NON-SMOKING?

NON, HE SAID WITH JUST A LITTLE SMUG SELF-RIGHTEOUSNESS.

GUM CHEWING OR NON-GUM CHEWING?

NON.

Zeke's Slop Stop

SMELLY FEET OR NON-SMELLY FEET?

NON.

Zeke's Slop Stop

SNORING OR NON-SNORING?

NON.

SOUP SLURPING OR NON-SOUP SLURPING? SINUS SNORTING OR NON-SINUS SNORTING? ODORIFEROUS BELCHING OR NON-ODORIFEROUS BELCHING?

NON!! NON! NON!

Zeke's Slop Stop

BIG-NOSED OR NON-BIG-NOSED?

UH...

Zeke's Slop Stop

WELL THIS IS A FINE HOW-DO-YOU-DO.

I WONDER IF YOU'D MIND PUTTING YOUR NOSE OUT WHILE I EAT?

SOUP

BIG NOSED

NON-BIG NOSED

107

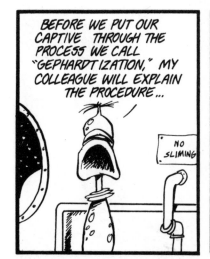

114

Panel 1: STEVE DALLAS HAD PASSED ON WITHOUT A WILL. A MEMBER OF HIS WAKE WAS THUS DISPATCHED TO FETCH HIS EARTHLY BOOTY.

STEVE'S STUFF

Panel 2: IT INCLUDED: LAW BOOKS, A FRAT PIN, LOOSE CHANGE AND A BOTTLE OF "OLD SPICE," WHICH PORTNOY ACCIDENTALLY DRANK, CAUSING HIM TO RUN AROUND THINKING HE WAS "AUNT BEA."

ANDY? OPIE??

Panel 3: A BOX OF TROJANS WAS ALSO FOUND AND, AFTER MUCH DEBATE, FINALLY IDENTIFIED AS POSSIBLY BEING MICRO-WAVE JELL-O MOLDS.

HMM.
BUT HE HATED COOKING!

STEVE'S STUFF

Panel 4: THE LATTER WERE FILLED WITH WATER AND DELIVERED AIRBORNE UNTO MRS. PAULA PEGWHISTLE'S PASSING PONTIAC... WHICH PRETTY WELL WRAPPED THINGS THE HECK UP FOR THE NIGHT.

BLAM!

Panel 5: STEVIE, STEVIE! STEVIE, STEVIE! ...WE HARDLY KNEW YE!

SNIFF!

Panel 6: SAY... WHAT'S THAT UP THERE? AN ALIEN SPACECRAFT?!

Panel 7: SSHHKKK!

Panel 8: ≩GULP!≩ S-STEVE?

JEEPERS! WHAT HAPPENED?

... TO BE CONTINUED! OR MAYBE IT WON'T! YA NEVER KNOW, DO YA?

Panel 9: I HEARD THE ALIENS GAVE STEVE BACK! LEMME SEE HIM!!

HE'S...HE'S RESTING. HE'S NOT EXACTLY HIMSELF AT THE MOMENT...

Panel 10: NO, NO! I'M UP, FELLAS! SAY...WHAT A BEAUTIFUL, BEAUTIFUL MORNING THIS IS!

Panel 11: WHAT ARE THOSE THINGS ON HIS FACE?

WHAT THINGS?

Panel 12: THOSE BROWN, THOUGHTFUL GLOBS!

HIS EYES!

ANYONE FOR CHURCH?

→ AND NOW A BRIEF DEMONSTRATION OF EMERGENCY MEDICAL TECHNIQUES FOR THE AMATEUR...

FOR CHOKING PERSONS:

"THE HEIMLICH MANEUVER"

GRASP VICTIM UNDER RIB CAGE AND SQUEEZE LIKE ALL GET-OUT. PARTIALLY CHEWED MEATBALL WILL BE EJECTED FROM ESOPHAGUS ONTO LOUD FAT MAN AT NEXT TABLE.

FOR DROWNING VICTIMS WHO HAVE TURNED BLUE:

"THE EISENBACHT MANEUVER"

PINCH VICTIM'S NOSE AND BLOW INTO HIS MOUTH UNTIL HE'S MAUVE.

PHEWW

FOR ELDERLY WOMEN WEARING LIME-GREEN PANTSUITS:

"THE HEIRENCHTSTERN MANEUVER"

TACKLE VICTIM AND STUFF SWATCHES OF STONE-WASHED DENIM UNDER ARMPITS UNTIL APPROVED LEVEL OF GOOD TASTE ENTERS BLOODSTREAM.

SHWACK!

FOR MEN WHO SIT ON THE EDGE OF NO-SMOKING AREAS AND SMOKE CIGARS THAT SMELL LIKE LARRY BIRD'S FEET:

"THE HEINEKENSTEICHKT MANEUVER"

HANG VICTIM FROM TOP OF THE WORLD TRADE CENTER AND LEGGO.

SOMETIMES YA JUST GOTTA SEIZE THE BULL BY THE HORNS OF A DILEMMA!

FOR INDIVIDUALS WHO CONSTANTLY MIX THEIR METAPHORS AND NEVER REALIZE IT:

"THE ROSEBUDEINLICHT MANEUVER"

BITE THEM.

I SEEM TO BE BETWEEN A ROCK AND A HARD PLACE IN THE SUN!

HELLO! THE CAPTAIN IS UNDER ATTACK FROM ANOTHER FEARSOME RUBY-LIPPED TONSIL SUCKER!

I SHALL MOVE IN TO ASSIST!

CAPTAIN! THE AFOREMENTIONED TONSIL SUCKER HAS ATTACHED HERSELF TO YOUR FACE! IF YOU WISH ASSISTANCE, PLEASE INDICATE BY COSMIC CODE!!

SMACK! SMOOCH SMOOCH! MMPH!

TRANSLATED, HE SAID, "BUG OFF."

HE BETTER WATCH HIMSELF...

...JIM BAKKER, JIMMY SWAGGART, WILBUR MILLS, GARY HART... ALL POWERFUL CAPTAINS BROUGHT DOWN BY TANGLING WITH A NONSANCTIONED RUBY-LIPPED SHE-CREATURE.

YEAH? WELL, WHAT I WANNA KNOW IS, WHAT BRINGS DOWN ONE OF THEM?! LIKE PAT SCHROEDER?

TEARS.

THIS SOUNDS LIKE A BAD FIFTIES MONSTER MOVIE.

WE'VE COME SO FAR.

HI, MA. SWEET BABY JESUS!

YOU REMEMBERED A LONELY MOTHER'S BIRTHDAY? MADE YOU A CARD, TOO. I DREW YOU AND ME HOLDING HANDS.

STEVEN MILHOUSE DALLAS... YOU GET YOUR BRAIN ZAPPED BY ALIENS OR SOMETHING? I'LL COOK UP A HAM, MA.

FIRE BACK®→

"WHERE THE READERS RESPOND"

—

TODAY:
MR. CHARLES RAYMOND FOXWORTH... PRESIDENT OF THE AMERICAN ASSOC. FOR THE ADVANCEMENT OF PEOPLE WITH FACIAL HAIR.

LAST WEEK, THIS FEATURE DISPLAYED A BEARDED PERSON CHARACTERIZED AS A VIOLENT LUNATIC. THIS IS PURE, IRRESPONSIBLE BIGOTRY.

PEOPLE WITH FACIAL HAIR ARE OFTEN DOCTORS, JUDGES, BAGGAGE HANDLERS AND OTHER LAW-ABIDING CITIZENS. WE STRONGLY RESENT THE STEREOTYPE SUGGESTING OTHERWISE.

"FIRE BACK®" WELCOMES OPPOSING VIEWPOINTS. WRITE ℅ THIS NEWSPAPER.

"...IN FACT, THIS SORT OF THING MAKES ME SO MAD I COULD STRANGLE A MANATEE IN THE NUDE..." AARGH..

THERE GOES ESTHER NEWBERG. BOY... YA KNOW WHAT THEY SAY ABOUT GIRLS WHO DON'T SHAVE... DON'T SAY IT.

WHAT? THAT THEY WEAR CAMOUFLAGE BOXER SHORTS? NOW YOU'VE DONE IT!

FIRE BACK®→

"WHERE THE READERS RESPOND"

—

TODAY:
MS. LINDA NUMMERS, SPOKESPERSON FOR THE UNITED DEFENSE FRONT FOR THE UNSHORN SISTERS OF THE APOCALYPSE.

STEREOTYPES: THE LANGUAGE OF HATE...

120

121

THE X-17 STEALTH BASSELOPE

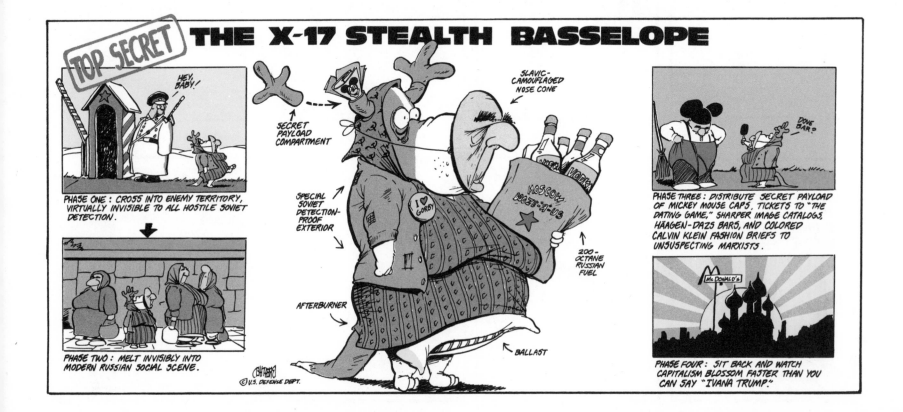